Hi _____,

I wrote a book about you. But (surprise!) you helped write it too. How did that happen? Well, basically you are the greatest friend in the history of friendships, so I just had to capture that greatness in this book and include all the things we'll want to remember forever.

And you know what? It turned out pretty awesome. Which shouldn't be a surprise at all because, in my book, you're seriously pretty awesome too.

Cheers to you!

_____

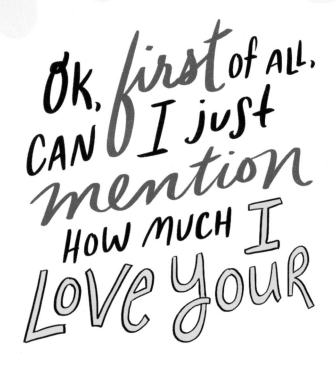

It's definitely ONE of YOUR SUPERPOWERS.

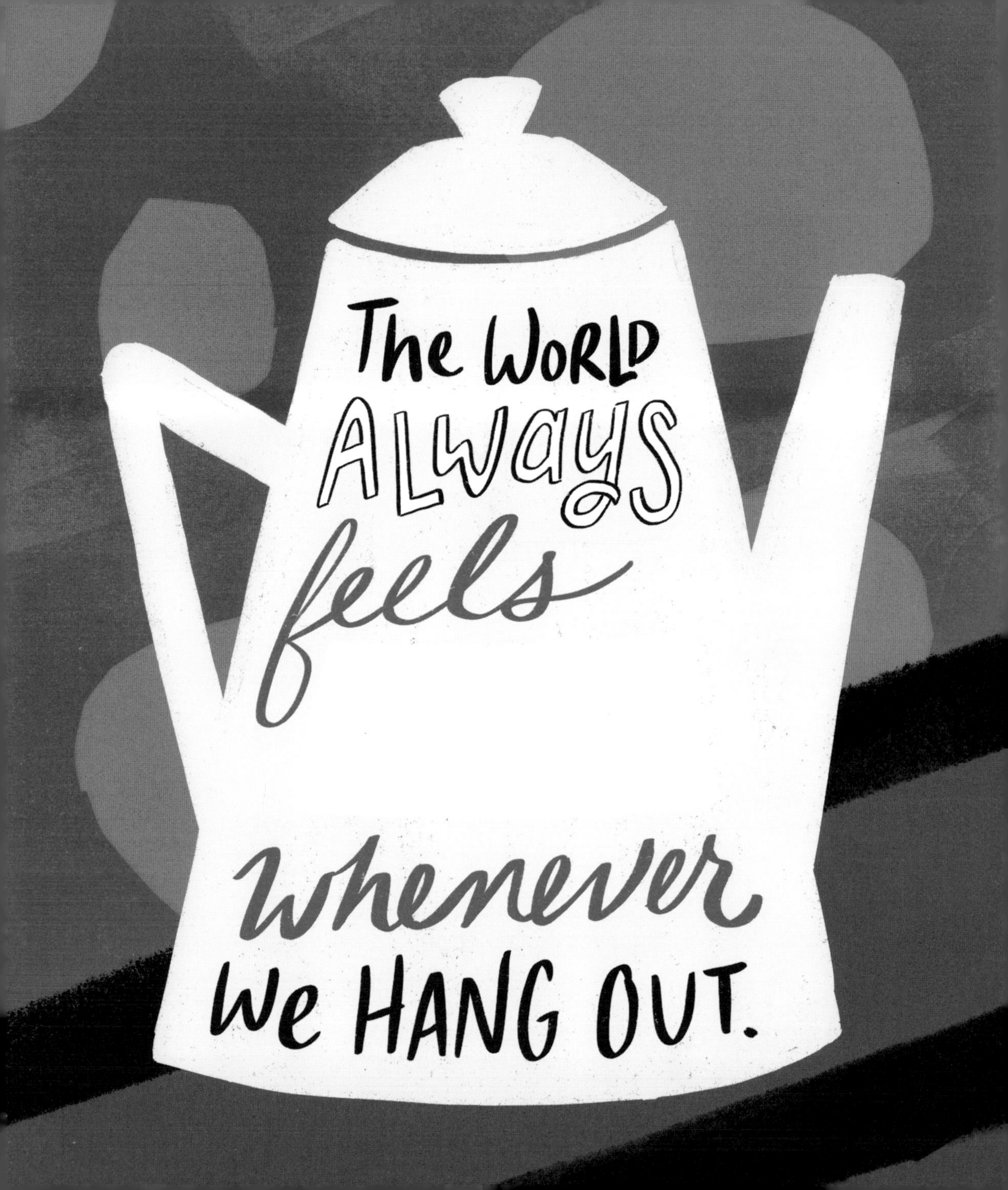
The WORLD
ALWAYS
feels
whenever
we HANG OUT.

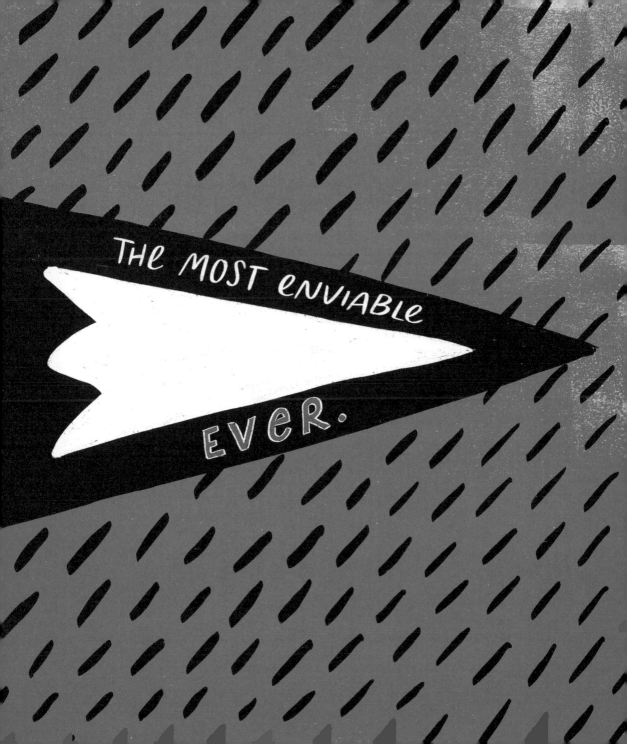

WOULDN'T YOU agree?

You're the ONLY PERSON IN THE *world* WHO CAN

you
inspire
me to

One of the
greatest
Gifts you
Give to the
World is

Let's say they make a movie about our friendship...

You'd be PLayed by:

I'd be PLayed by:

AND the WHOLE thing WOULD JUST BE ABOUT how IMPRESSIVE WE ARE!

I don't Really KNOW how you and

at the SaMe TiMe.
(Do you have a stunt double?)

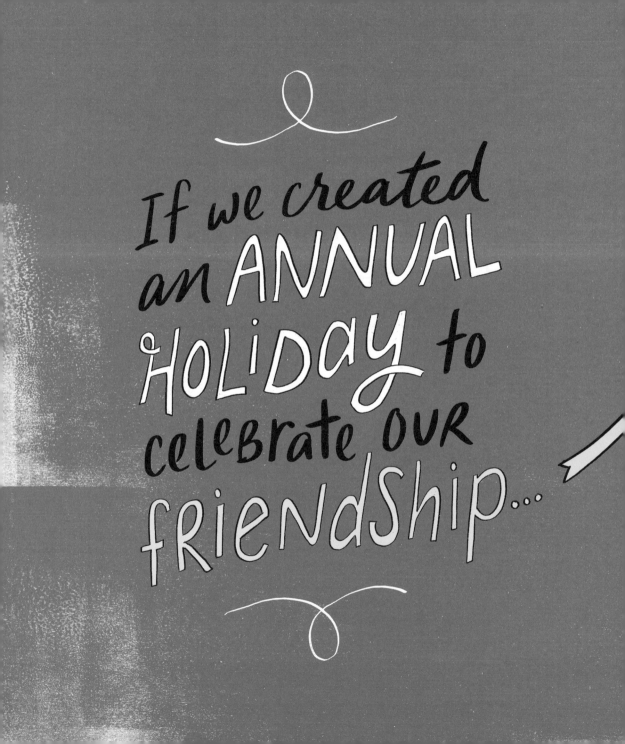

If we created an ANNUAL HOLIDAY to celebrate our friendShip...

It would be called
_____ .

We would always
eat things like
_____ ,

and we'd spend our
time _____

_____ .

You know,
I secretly
ADMiRe
HOW YOU

If we were a GAME, we'd Be:

If we were a PAIR of SHOES, we'd Be:

If we were a BAND, we'd Be:

The way you _____ deserves an OLYMPIC GOLD MEDAL.

I almost
COULDN'T BELIEVE it.
But I *also* happen
TO KNOW JUST
HOW INCREDIBLE
YOU ARE.

if everyone could

Like you.

I love that you're
the ONLY ONE
who understands my

And that I'm
the ONLY ONE
who *understands* YOUR

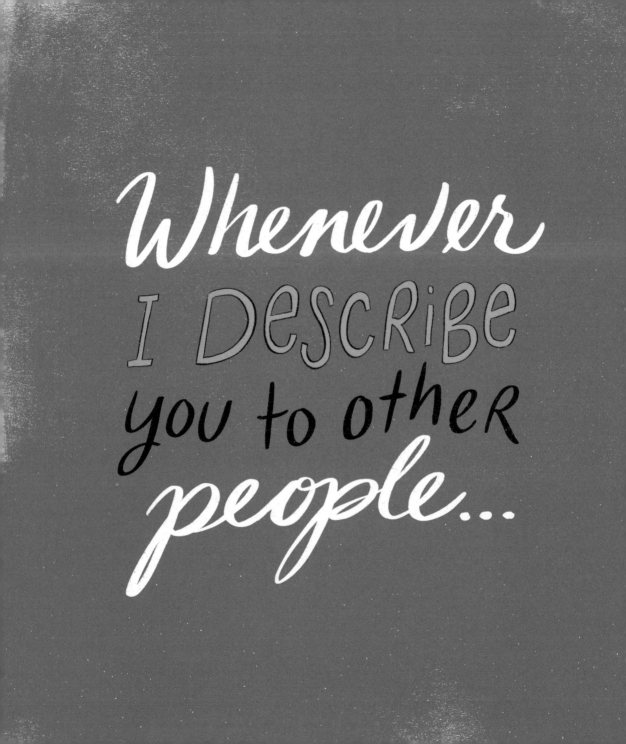

Whenever I Describe you to other people...

I ALWAYS
Say that you're

Because it's
TRUE.

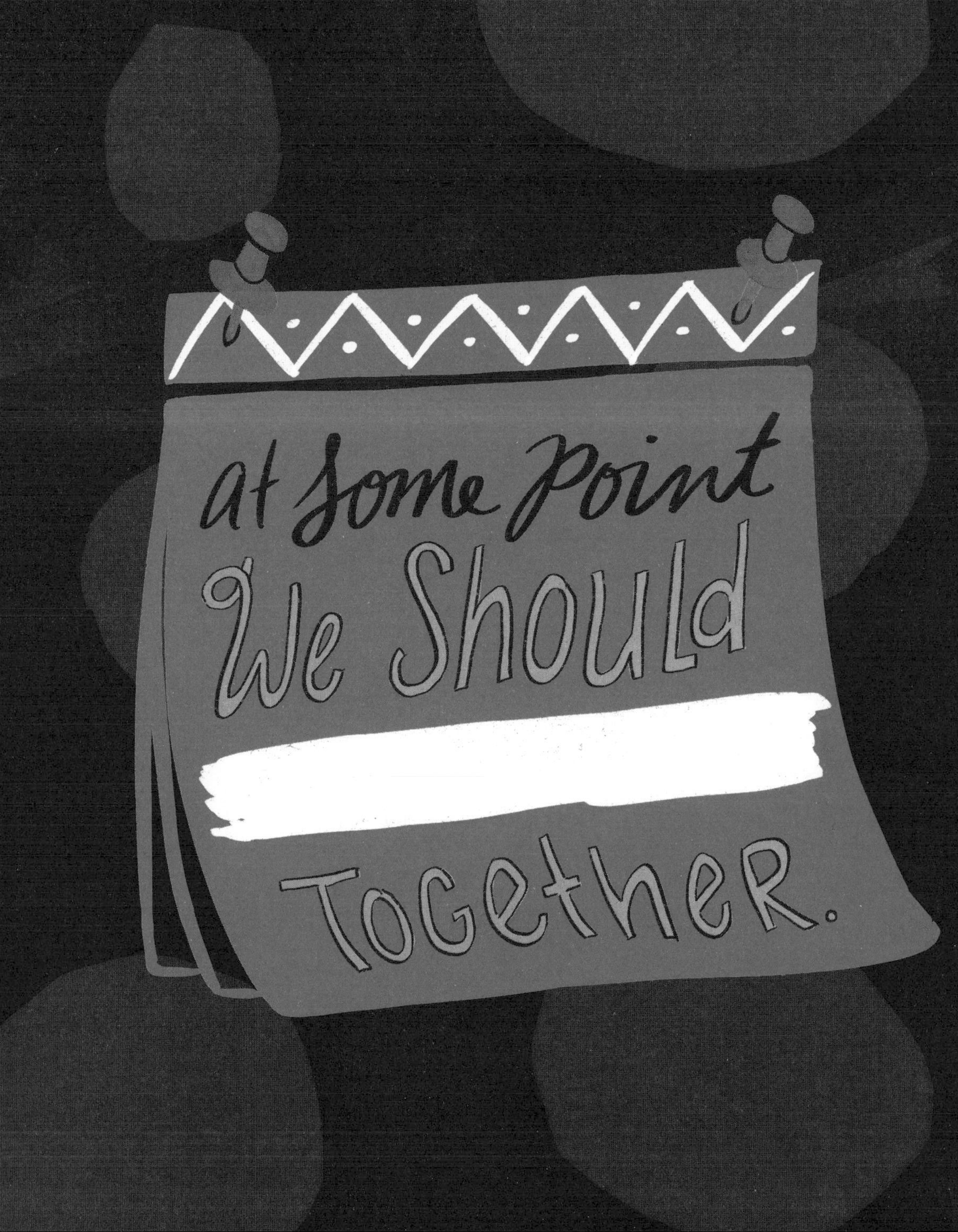
at Some Point
We Should
Together.

Let's
put it on the
calendar.

HERE ARE SOME THINGS WE CAN PUT IN IT:

_____

_____

_____

_____

_____

_____

But you *always* SEEM TO

(HOW DO YOU DO THAT?)

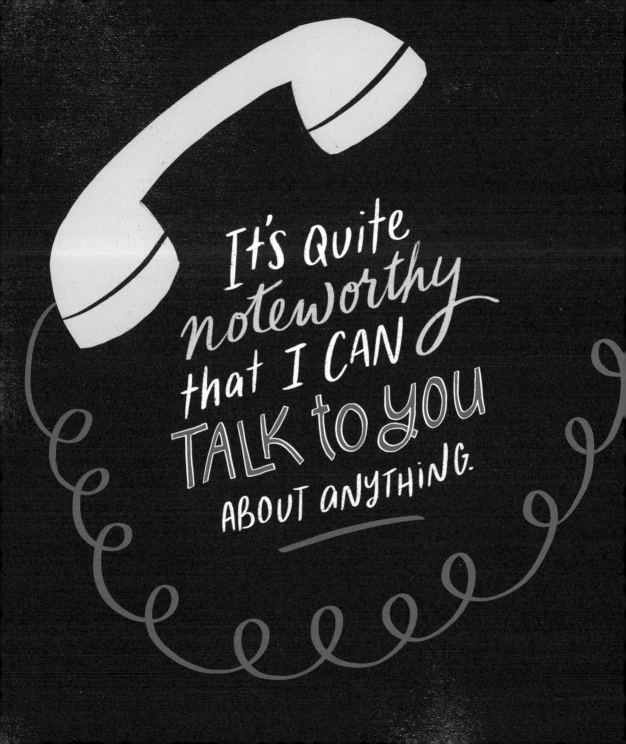

EVEN SIMPLE
things like

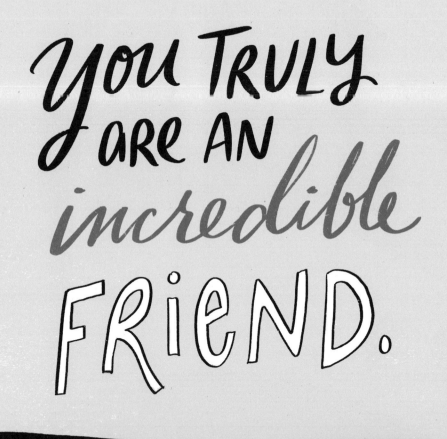

COMPENDIUM®
live inspired

Actually
WRITTEN BY:

WRITTEN BY: Miriam Hathaway

DESIGNED AND ILLUSTRATED BY: Justine Edge

EDITED BY: Ruth Austin

Library of Congress Control Number: 2018955822 | ISBN: 978-1-946-873-57-6

5th printing. Printed in China with soy and metallic inks on FSC®-Mix certified paper.

Create meaningful moments with gifts that inspire.

CONNECT WITH US
live-inspired.com | sayhello@compendiuminc.com

@compendiumliveinspired
#compendiumliveinspired